Faster Than Takeout: 20-Minute Chinese Dishes
A Chinese Takeout Cookbook for Busy Nights

Peter Ouyang

Book Design -
www.socialbuzagency.com/freedompublishing

Thank you for choosing my book. It was a labor of love and I poured my heart and soul into making it as special as possible. As a thank you, I would like to offer you a $500 gift certificate to use with Freedom Publishing, the company that helped me bring my dream of publishing to life.

Years ago, I never thought I would have the ability to publish a book, but thanks to Amazon and the amazing team at Freedom Publishing, I was able to make it a reality. As a small family-owned business, my goal has always been to provide the best Chinese recipes to people across the country who purchase my book.

With Amazon and Freedom Publishing, my family now lives life on our own terms, and I am grateful for the opportunity to travel and spend time with my loved ones.

If you ever dream of creating your own book business, Freedom Publishing has everything you need, from graphic designers to ghostwriters and book editors. The $500 gift certificate can be used towards a consultation session to get started.

The team at Freedom Publishing is knowledgeable, kind, and professional, and they love helping everyday people build their own book businesses. If it wasn't for Amazon and Freedom Publishing, we would still be working our 9 to 5 jobs and not have time for our kids.

I hope to one day purchase your book on Amazon and help you achieve your dreams.

Thank you again for choosing my book.

P.S. Be sure to let them know who sent you.. We have a great relationship and they will do their very best to help you.

Table of Contents

IV. Conclusion

Brief history of Chinese cuisine

The history of Chinese cuisine is a rich tapestry of flavors, ingredients, and cultural influences. Spanning thousands of years, Chinese cuisine has evolved over time to become one of the world's most beloved and diverse culinary traditions. From the imperial banquets of the Han dynasty to the regional specialties of modern-day China, Chinese cuisine has always been a reflection of the culture and history of the country.

The earliest evidence of Chinese cuisine dates to the Neolithic period, when people relied on hunting, fishing, and gathering for their food. However, it was during the Han dynasty (206 BCE - 220 CE) that food became a symbol of social status and wealth, leading to the creation of elaborate banquets and the introduction of new ingredients and cooking techniques. The court of the Han dynasty was renowned for its lavish feasts, which included dishes like steamed and roasted meats, soups, and vegetable dishes.

The Tang dynasty (618-907 CE) saw the rise of trade with the West, which brought new spices and flavors to China, further expanding the culinary landscape. During this time, the capital city of Chang'an (modern-day Xi'an) was considered one of the culinary capitals of the world, with street food vendors and dining establishments offering a wide variety of dishes to satisfy any palate. The cuisine of the Tang dynasty was also heavily influenced by the cuisines of neighboring countries, leading to the creation of dishes like noodle soups and stir-fry dishes.

In the Ming dynasty (1368-1644 CE), the imperial court continued to refine and elevate Chinese cuisine, leading to the creation of famous dishes like Peking duck. During this time, culinary arts became a highly regarded profession, and chefs from around the country came to the capital to showcase their skills. The imperial court also continued to influence the development of regional cuisines, with each province developing its own unique dishes and flavors.

Today, Chinese cuisine is known for its diverse regional styles, which reflect the local ingredients and cultural influences of each area. From the spicy Sichuan cuisine in the southwest to the Cantonese cuisine of Guangdong province, each region has its own distinct dishes and flavors. The use of ingredients like rice, noodles, seafood, and meats like pork and beef is common throughout the country, and the cuisine is known for its use of seasonings like ginger, garlic, and soy sauce.

In conclusion, the history of Chinese cuisine is a rich and diverse story of cultural exchange, innovation, and the evolution of flavors and ingredients. From its humble beginnings as a simple subsistence diet, Chinese cuisine has grown to become one of the world's most beloved and diverse culinary traditions, reflecting the history, culture, and diversity of the country itself.

Overview of Chinese cooking techniques

Culinary traditions of China are the rich and diverse. From stir-frying to steaming, roasting to boiling, Chinese cooking techniques have been honed and perfected over thousands of years to create the delicious and complex flavors that are the hallmark of this cuisine.

One of the most fundamental techniques in Chinese cooking is stir-frying. Stir-frying is a quick and efficient method of cooking that involves heating a small amount of oil in a wok or frying pan over high heat and stirring the ingredients constantly to ensure even cooking. This technique is ideal for cooking small pieces of food, like vegetables or meat, and allows the ingredients to retain their texture, color, and flavor. Stir-frying is often used in dishes like kung pao chicken and moo shu pork.

Another common cooking technique in Chinese cuisine is steaming. Steaming is a gentle method of cooking that involves placing food in a steamer basket over boiling water and cooking until it is tender and flavorful. This technique is ideal for delicate ingredients like fish, dumplings, and buns, and helps to preserve their natural flavors and nutrients. Steaming is often used in dishes like steamed fish and steamed buns.

Roasting is another important technique in Chinese cooking and is often used to create crispy and flavorful dishes like roast pork and Peking duck. Roasting involves cooking food in an oven or over an open flame until it is golden brown and crispy on the outside and tender and juicy on the inside. Roasting is a time-consuming method, but the end result is well worth the effort.

Finally, boiling is a simple yet effective cooking technique that is often used in Chinese cuisine to create soups, broths, and stews. Boiling involves cooking ingredients in a pot of boiling water until they are tender and flavorful. This technique is ideal for ingredients like noodles, dumplings, and vegetables, and allows the flavors of the ingredients to infuse the broth or soup. Boiling is often used in dishes like hot and sour soup and wonton soup.

In conclusion, Chinese cooking techniques are an essential part of this rich and diverse cuisine, and are a testament to the ingenuity and creativity of Chinese chefs. Whether stir-frying, steaming, roasting, or boiling, these techniques are used to create the delicious and complex flavors that are the hallmark of this cuisine, and are an essential part of the professional chef's toolkit.

Essential ingredients for Chinese cooking.

Soy Sauce

Soy sauce, a staple condiment in Chinese cuisine, is an essential ingredient in many dishes and has been used for centuries by Chinese chiefs to add flavor and depth to their creations.

Soy sauce is made from fermented soybeans and wheat, and the traditional method of production can take several months. The sauce is then aged to produce its unique taste and aroma.

In Chinese cooking, soy sauce is used in a variety of ways to enhance the flavors of different dishes. For example, it can be used as a marinade for meat, poultry, and fish, or as a base for sauces and dips.

One of the most common ways that Chinese chiefs use soy sauce is in stir-fry dishes. This popular cooking technique involves quickly cooking small pieces of food over high heat while continuously stirring. Soy sauce is often added towards the end of the cooking process to add flavor and create a rich, savory sauce.

Another way that soy sauce is used in Chinese cooking is in soups and broths. The sauce is often added to the broth at the beginning of the cooking process to infuse the liquid with its rich, umami flavor.

In addition to its use in cooking, soy sauce can also be used as a dipping sauce for dumplings, spring rolls, and other fried foods. It is also a common ingredient in sauces and marinades for grilled and roasted meats.

In conclusion, soy sauce is a versatile and essential ingredient in Chinese cuisine. Whether it is used to enhance the flavor of a stir-fry, to add depth to a soup or broth, or as a dipping sauce for dumplings, soy sauce has been an important part of Chinese cooking for centuries. And it continues to be a favorite among Chinese chiefs and diners alike.

Rice Vinegar

Rice vinegar is a staple ingredient in Chinese cuisine, prized for its mild and slightly sweet flavor. Chinese chiefs use rice vinegar in a variety of ways to add depth and brightness to their dishes.

Rice vinegar is made by fermenting rice wine and has a slightly milder and sweeter taste compared to other types of vinegar. It is often used as a condiment and ingredient in Chinese cooking, and is especially popular in dishes such as stir-fries, salads, and pickled vegetables.

One of the most common uses of rice vinegar by Chinese chiefs is in stir-fry dishes. A splash of rice vinegar added towards the end of the cooking process helps to brighten the flavors of the dish and balance the richness of other ingredients, such as soy sauce or oyster sauce.

Rice vinegar is also used to make dipping sauces for dumplings, steamed buns, and other dim sum dishes. The mild flavor of rice vinegar pairs well with soy sauce, ginger, and garlic to create a simple, yet delicious dipping sauce.

In addition to its use in cooking, rice vinegar is also used to make pickled vegetables. This ancient preservation method involves marinating vegetables in a mixture of rice vinegar, sugar, and salt. The resulting pickled vegetables are crunchy, tangy, and full of flavor, and are often served as a side dish or snack.

Another use of rice vinegar by Chinese chefs is in marinades for meats and poultry. A mixture of rice vinegar, soy sauce, and other ingredients is used to tenderize and flavor the meat, resulting in a delicious and juicy dish.

In conclusion, rice vinegar is an essential ingredient in Chinese cuisine, used by Chinese chiefs to add depth, brightness, and balance to their dishes. Whether it is used in stir-fries, dipping sauces, pickled vegetables, or marinades, rice vinegar is a versatile ingredient that has been used for centuries to enhance the flavors of Chinese cuisine.

Sesame Oil

Sesame oil is a staple ingredient in Chinese cuisine, used for its rich, nutty flavor and aroma. Chinese chiefs use sesame oil in a variety of ways to add depth and richness to their dishes.

Sesame oil is made from toasted or raw sesame seeds and has a strong, distinctive flavor that pairs well with other ingredients in Chinese cooking. The oil is often used in small quantities to enhance the flavor of sauces, marinades, and stir-fry dishes.

One of the most common uses of sesame oil by Chinese chiefs is in stir-fry dishes. A small amount of sesame oil added towards the end of the cooking process provides a nutty flavor that complements the flavors of the other ingredients in the dish.

Sesame oil is also used to make sauces and marinades for meats and poultry. A mixture of sesame oil, soy sauce, rice vinegar, and other ingredients is used to flavor and tenderize the meat, resulting in a delicious and juicy dish.

In addition to its use in cooking, sesame oil is also used in dressings for salads and cold dishes. A small amount of sesame oil added to a dressing provides a nutty flavor that pairs well with ingredients such as vinegar, soy sauce, and ginger.

Another use of sesame oil by Chinese chefs is in soups and broths. A small amount of sesame oil added to the broth at the beginning of the cooking process provides a rich, nutty flavor that infuses the entire soup.

In conclusion, sesame oil is a versatile and essential ingredient in Chinese cuisine. Used by Chinese chiefs in small quantities to add depth and richness to their dishes, sesame oil is an important part of many traditional Chinese recipes. Whether it is used in stir-fries, sauces, marinades, dressings, or soups, sesame oil is a staple ingredient that has been used for centuries to enhance the flavors of Chinese cuisine.

Ginger

Ginger is a staple ingredient in Chinese cuisine, used for its pungent flavor and numerous health benefits. Chinese chefs use ginger in a variety of ways to add depth and spice to their dishes.

Ginger is a root vegetable that has been used in Chinese cooking for thousands of years. It has a pungent, slightly sweet flavor that pairs well with other ingredients such as soy sauce, garlic, and scallions.

One of the most common uses of ginger by Chinese chefs is in stir-fry dishes. Ginger is often sliced or minced and added to the pan early in the cooking process, infusing the dish with its unique flavor. Ginger is particularly popular in dishes that feature seafood, poultry, or beef.

Ginger is also used in marinades for meats and poultry. A mixture of ginger, soy sauce, rice vinegar, and other ingredients is used to flavor and tenderize the meat, resulting in a delicious and juicy dish.

In addition to its use in cooking, ginger is also used in soups and broths. A small amount of sliced or grated ginger added to the broth at the beginning of the cooking process provides a warming flavor that infuses the entire soup.

Another use of ginger by Chinese chefs is in sweet and savory desserts. Fresh ginger is often grated and used to make ginger candy or added to sweet syrups for use in ginger-infused desserts.

In conclusion, ginger is a versatile and essential ingredient in Chinese cuisine. Used by Chinese chefs in a variety of dishes to add depth and spice, ginger is an important part of many traditional Chinese recipes. Whether it is used in stir-fries, marinades, soups, or desserts, ginger is a staple ingredient that has been used for centuries to enhance the flavors of Chinese cuisine.

Garlic

Garlic is a staple ingredient in Chinese cuisine, used for its pungent flavor and numerous health benefits.

Chinese chefs use garlic in a variety of ways to add depth and aroma to their dishes.

Garlic is a pungent bulb that has been used in Chinese cooking for thousands of years. It has a strong, slightly sweet flavor that pairs well with other ingredients such as ginger, soy sauce, and scallions.

One of the most common uses of garlic by Chinese chefs is in stir-fry dishes. Garlic is often minced or sliced and added to the pan early in the cooking process, infusing the dish with its unique flavor. Garlic is particularly popular in dishes that feature meats, poultry, or seafood.

Garlic is also used in sauces for dipping and marinades for meats and poultry. A mixture of garlic, soy sauce, rice vinegar, and other ingredients is used to flavor and tenderize the meat, resulting in a delicious and juicy dish.

In addition to its use in cooking, garlic is also used in soups and broths. A small amount of minced or sliced garlic added to the broth at the beginning of the cooking process provides a pungent flavor that infuses the entire soup.

Another use of garlic by Chinese chefs is in cold dishes such as salads and pickles. Garlic is often minced or sliced and added to the dish to provide a pungent flavor that pairs well with vinegar, soy sauce, and ginger.

In conclusion, garlic is a versatile and essential ingredient in Chinese cuisine. Used by Chinese chefs in a variety of dishes to add depth and aroma, garlic is an important part of many traditional Chinese recipes. Whether it is used in stir-fries, sauces, marinades, soups, or cold dishes, garlic is a staple ingredient that has been used for centuries to enhance the flavors of Chinese cuisine.

Scallions

Scallions, also known as green onions or spring onions, are an integral part of Chinese cuisine. They are widely used to add flavor and aroma to dishes, as well as to provide a decorative touch to the finished dish. Chinese chefs have long appreciated the versatility of scallions, incorporating them into a wide range of dishes, from stir-fries to soups to steamed dumplings.

One of the most popular uses of scallions in Chinese cooking is in stir-fries. Scallions are often sliced thin and added to the pan near the end of the cooking process, providing a bright, crisp flavor that complements the other ingredients in the dish. For example, scallions are often used in stir-fries with beef, chicken, or seafood, to add a fresh burst of flavor to the dish.

Another common use of scallions in Chinese cooking is in soups. The tender white parts of the scallions are finely chopped and added to the broth, while the green parts are used to garnish the finished soup. This not only adds flavor but also provides a pop of color to the soup.

Steamed dishes such as dumplings and buns are also often flavored with scallions. Chopped scallions are mixed into the dough or filling, providing a subtle onion flavor that complements the other ingredients. This is particularly common in northern Chinese cuisine, where scallions are used extensively in steamed dumplings and buns.

In addition to their use in cooking, scallions are also often used in marinades, dipping sauces, and other seasonings in Chinese cuisine. They are known for their ability to add a fresh, pungent flavor to dishes, without overpowering the other ingredients. For example, a simple scallion sauce can be made by mixing chopped scallions with soy sauce, vinegar, and sesame oil, to create a versatile condiment that can be used with a wide range of dishes.

In conclusion, scallions are an indispensable ingredient in Chinese cuisine, providing flavor, aroma, and color to a wide range of dishes. Whether they are added to stir-fries, soups, or steamed dishes, scallions are always a welcome addition to any meal, elevating the flavors of the dish and providing a unique, fresh taste. Whether you are a seasoned Chinese chef or a home cook, scallions should always be a staple in your kitchen.

Hoisin Sauce

Hoisin sauce is a staple ingredient in Chinese cuisine, used in a variety of dishes to add depth of flavor and sweetness. Originating from the Guangdong province in southern China, hoisin sauce is made from fermented soybeans, sugar, garlic, and spices. The resulting thick, sticky sauce is used as a dipping sauce, a marinade, or a stir-fry sauce.

One of the most popular dishes that utilize hoisin sauce is Peking duck. The sauce is brushed onto the crispy skin of the duck before serving, adding a sweet and savory element to the dish. Another popular dish that incorporates hoisin sauce is moo shu pork. In this dish, hoisin sauce is used as a dipping sauce for the pancakes that wrap around the stir-fried pork, vegetables, and mushrooms.

In addition to being a key ingredient in traditional dishes, hoisin sauce is also a versatile addition to other Chinese-inspired dishes. It can be used in stir-fries, sauces for meat and seafood, or as a glaze for grilled meats and vegetables. The rich, sweet flavor of hoisin sauce pairs well with the bold flavors of ginger, garlic, and soy sauce, making it a popular ingredient in many Chinese-style sauces and marinades.

Hoisin sauce is also a popular condiment in many Asian-style restaurants, often served alongside other dipping sauces such as soy sauce and chili paste. The versatility of hoisin sauce makes it a favorite among Chinese chefs, who use it to enhance the flavor of a wide range of dishes.

In conclusion, hoisin sauce is an integral part of Chinese cuisine, adding depth of flavor and sweetness to a variety of dishes. From traditional dishes like Peking duck to modern fusion cuisine, hoisin sauce is a versatile and beloved ingredient in the Chinese culinary tradition.

Shaoxing Wine

Shaoxing wine is a staple ingredient in Chinese cuisine, used to add depth of flavor to dishes and to tenderize meats. It is a type of rice wine that originates from the city of Shaoxing in the Zhejiang province of China. Shaoxing wine is made from fermented rice, yeast, and water, and has a sweet, rich, and slightly nutty flavor.

In cooking, Shaoxing wine is often used to marinate meats such as chicken, beef, and pork. The wine helps to break down the meat fibers, making it tender and juicy. It is also used to deglaze pans, adding flavor to sauces and gravies. A splash of Shaoxing wine is also commonly added to stir-fry dishes to enhance the flavor of the ingredients.

One of the most famous dishes that uses Shaoxing wine is the traditional Chinese dish of braised pork belly, known as "red-cooked pork." In this dish, the pork is slow-cooked in a mixture of Shaoxing wine, soy sauce, ginger, garlic, and spices, resulting in a rich and flavorful dish. Shaoxing wine is also used in the classic Chinese dish of drunken chicken, in which the chicken is marinated in the wine overnight before being steamed or boiled.

In addition to being used in cooking, Shaoxing wine is also a popular ingredient in Chinese-style marinades and sauces. The rich, nutty flavor of the wine pairs well with soy sauce, ginger, and garlic, making it a popular ingredient in many Chinese-style dipping sauces and marinades.

In conclusion, Shaoxing wine is an essential ingredient in Chinese cuisine, adding depth of flavor to dishes and tenderizing meats. From classic dishes like red-cooked pork to modern fusion cuisine, Shaoxing wine is a versatile and beloved ingredient in the Chinese culinary tradition. Whether used in cooking, as a marinade, or in sauces, Shaoxing wine is an important part of the rich and diverse culinary heritage of China.

Cornstarch

Cornstarch is a staple ingredient in Chinese cuisine, used to thicken sauces, marinades, and soups, as well as to coat meats for stir-frying and deep-frying. Cornstarch is made from the endosperm of corn kernels and is a fine, white powder that is easily dissolved in liquid.

In cooking, cornstarch is often used to thicken sauces, such as in the classic Chinese dish of sweet and sour pork. In this dish, a mixture of cornstarch and water is added to a sauce made of vinegar, sugar, and ketchup, resulting in a thick, glossy sauce that clings to the tender, crispy-fried pork. Cornstarch is also commonly used to make stir-fry sauces, such as in the classic dish of kung pao chicken. In this dish, a mixture of cornstarch, water, soy sauce, and vinegar is added to the pan, thickening the sauce and glazing the chicken and vegetables.

In addition to being used as a thickener, cornstarch is also commonly used to coat meats before stir-frying or deep-frying. The cornstarch helps to create a crispy exterior on the meat, while also preventing it from sticking to the pan or becoming too dry during cooking. A popular example of this technique is the classic dish of General Tso's chicken. In this dish, chicken pieces are coated in a mixture of cornstarch and flour before being deep-fried, resulting in a crispy, juicy, and flavorful dish.

Cornstarch is also used in soups, such as in the classic Chinese dish of hot and sour soup. In this dish, a small amount of cornstarch is added to the soup at the end of cooking, thickening the broth and adding body to the soup.

In conclusion, cornstarch is a versatile and essential ingredient in Chinese cuisine. From thickening sauces to coating meats, cornstarch is a key component in many classic Chinese dishes. Its fine, white powder is easily dissolved in liquid, making it a convenient and reliable ingredient for Chinese chefs. Whether used in stir-fries, soups, or sauces, cornstarch is an important part of the rich and diverse culinary heritage of China.

Chili paste

Chili paste is a staple ingredient in Chinese cuisine, used to add heat and depth of flavor to dishes. Made from chili peppers, garlic, ginger, and other spices, chili paste is a spicy, flavorful condiment that is essential in many classic Chinese dishes.

In cooking, chili paste is often used to add heat to stir-fry dishes, such as mapo tofu and kung pao chicken. A small amount of chili paste is added to the pan, infusing the dish with a spicy kick. Chili paste is also used to make spicy dipping sauces, such as in the classic Chinese dish of hot and sour soup. In this dish, a mixture of chili paste, vinegar, and soy sauce is served on the side, allowing diners to adjust the heat to their liking.

Chili paste is also a popular ingredient in marinades, adding heat and flavor to meats such as chicken, beef, and pork. In the classic Chinese dish of Szechuan-style twice-cooked pork, sliced pork belly is stir-fried with chili paste, garlic, ginger, and Szechuan peppercorns, resulting in a spicy and flavorful dish.

In addition to being used in cooking, chili paste is also a popular ingredient in many Chinese-style sauces and condiments. A small spoonful of chili paste can be added to soy sauce to create a spicy dipping sauce, or to hot oil to make a fiery oil to drizzle over dishes.

In conclusion, chili paste is an essential ingredient in Chinese cuisine, adding heat and depth of flavor to dishes. From stir-fries to marinades to sauces, chili paste is a versatile and beloved ingredient in the Chinese culinary tradition. Whether used to add heat to classic dishes or to create spicy sauces, chili paste is an important part of the rich and diverse culinary heritage of China.

Kitchen Tools and Equipment:

(scan QR code for more information)

Wok

A wok is a versatile and essential tool in Chinese cooking, used for stir-frying, sautéing, deep-frying, and boiling. A chef can use a wok in several ways to prepare traditional Chinese dishes:

1. Stir-frying: Stir-frying is a common cooking method in Chinese cuisine where ingredients are quickly cooked over high heat. The wok's rounded shape

and high sides allow for fast and even heating, making it ideal for stir-frying.

2. Sautéing: Sautéing involves cooking food in a small amount of oil over high heat. The wok's wide surface area allows for ample room to cook and toss ingredients, making it a useful tool for sautéing.

3. Deep-frying: The wok's high sides and rounded shape make it an ideal pan for deep-frying. Its material, typically carbon steel, is durable and conductive, allowing for high heat, which is necessary for deep-frying.

4. Boiling: The wok can also be used for boiling, either as a pot to cook ingredients in, or as a shallow pan to blanch ingredients.

A chef may also use a wok to smoke ingredients, such as meats and tofu, by placing a small amount of smoky ingredients, such as tea leaves, in the wok and covering it with a lid. The smoky flavor imparts a unique and delicious taste to the food.

Overall, a wok is a versatile and essential tool in Chinese cooking, allowing for quick and efficient preparation of a wide range of dishes, from stir-fries to deep-fried foods.

Wok Spatula and Ladle

A wok spatula and ladle are essential tools for Chinese cooking because they are specifically designed for use with a wok. The wok spatula has a flat and wide surface, making it ideal for stir-frying and tossing ingredients in the wok. Its curved edge helps to scrape the bottom of the wok and prevent food from sticking. The ladle, on the other hand, is used for serving and transferring liquids and sauces, such as soups and broths. It is also useful for adding and measuring ingredients when cooking in a wok, as its shape and size are ideal for scooping and pouring. Together, a wok spatula and ladle help to make cooking in a wok efficient and effortless, allowing for precise and controlled handling of ingredients and liquids.

Rice cooker

A rice cooker is an essential tool for Chinese cooking because rice is a staple food in Chinese cuisine and cooking it correctly can be challenging. Rice cookers automate the cooking process and ensure that the rice is cooked evenly and to the desired consistency every time. The appliance has precise temperature control and a timer, so the rice can be cooked and held at the optimal temperature until ready to serve. This eliminates the need to monitor the pot on the stove and adjust the heat to prevent the rice from burning or becoming mushy. Additionally, many rice cookers have a "keep warm" function, which maintains the temperature of the cooked rice for several hours without drying it out, making it convenient for serving at any time. Overall, a rice cooker is a convenient and reliable tool for cooking perfect rice, a staple in Chinese cuisine.

Steamer basket

A steamer basket is commonly used in Chinese cooking to steam food, such as dim sum, dumplings, fish, and vegetables. The steamer basket fits inside a pot with boiling water, and the food is placed on the basket. The steam from the boiling water cooks the food, retaining its flavor, nutrients, and texture. The steamer basket is an ideal cooking method for delicate foods, as it does not expose the food to direct heat, which can cause it to dry out or become tough.

A chef may use a steamer basket in several ways in Chinese cooking:

1. To cook dim sum: Dim sum is often steamed and served in bamboo baskets. The steamer basket allows for quick and even cooking, producing perfectly steamed dumplings and buns.

2. To steam fish: Steaming fish is a popular way to cook it in Chinese cuisine. The steamer basket

helps to cook the fish evenly and gently, resulting in tender and flaky fish.

3. To cook vegetables: Steaming vegetables is a healthy and flavorful way to prepare them. The steamer basket allows the vegetables to retain their nutrients and bright colors while cooking evenly.

Overall, a steamer basket is a versatile and essential tool in Chinese cooking, allowing chefs to prepare a variety of dishes while preserving their natural flavors, textures, and nutrients.

Cleaver Knife

A cleaver knife is a staple tool in Chinese cooking, used for a variety of tasks, including chopping, slicing, and crushing. Its unique design, with a heavy blade and square tip, makes it versatile and useful in the kitchen.

A chef can use a cleaver knife in several ways in Chinese cooking:

1. Chopping: The cleaver knife is ideal for chopping meats, vegetables, and herbs, as its heavy blade allows for quick and efficient cutting.

2. Slicing: The cleaver knife can also be used for slicing meat and vegetables, making it a versatile tool for preparing ingredients for a wide range of dishes.

3. Crushing: The cleaver knife's square tip can be used to crush garlic, ginger, and other ingredients, making it an essential tool for mashing and grinding.

4. Cleaving: The cleaver knife is also useful for cleaving meat, poultry, and fish, allowing a chef to separate bones from meat and cut through joints.

Overall, a cleaver knife is a versatile and essential tool in Chinese cooking, allowing a chef to quickly and efficiently prepare a wide range of ingredients for a variety of dishes.

Cutting Board

A cutting board is a crucial tool in Chinese cooking, used to prepare ingredients for cooking. Here are some ways a chef may use a cutting board in Chinese cooking:

1. Cutting vegetables: The chef will use a cutting board to chop and slice vegetables, such as onions, carrots, bell peppers, and mushrooms, into small pieces for stir-frying or other dishes.

2. Dicing meat: The chef will use a cutting board to dice cooked meat, such as chicken, beef, or pork, into small pieces for stir-frying or other dishes.

3. Mincing garlic and ginger: The chef will use a cutting board to mince garlic and ginger, which are key ingredients in many Chinese dishes, to create a fine paste.

4. Preparing ingredients: The chef may use the cutting board to prepare other ingredients, such as cutting noodles or slicing meat.

It's important to use a clean, sanitary cutting board when preparing food, to minimize the risk of foodborne illness. A chef may use a separate cutting board for different types of food, such as one for vegetables, one for meat, and one for seafood, to prevent cross-contamination.

Chopsticks

Chopsticks are an important tool in Chinese cooking, used for several tasks in the kitchen. While they are most commonly associated with eating, chopsticks are also used as cooking utensils in Chinese cuisine.

A chef can use chopsticks in several ways in Chinese cooking:

1. Mixing and stirring: Chopsticks can be used to mix and stir ingredients in a wok or pot, allowing for quick and efficient cooking.

2. Tasting: Chopsticks can be used to taste food while it is cooking, allowing a chef to adjust the seasoning and flavor as needed.

3. Serving: Chopsticks can also be used to serve food, especially dishes that are too hot to touch with bare hands.

4. Handling hot food: Chopsticks can be used to handle hot food, such as stir-fried vegetables and meats, without burning the chef's hands.

Overall, chopsticks are an essential tool in Chinese cooking, allowing a chef to quickly and efficiently perform a variety of tasks, from mixing and tasting to serving and handling hot food.

20 recipes that can be done in 20 minutes.

Fried Rice:

Chinese Fried Rice is a classic Chinese dish that has become popular all over the world. It is a simple and versatile dish that can be made with a variety of ingredients and customized to individual tastes. The dish typically consists of cooked rice that is stir-fried with vegetables, meats, and eggs, and seasoned with soy sauce and other seasonings. The ingredients used in Chinese fried rice vary depending on the region and personal preferences, but some common ingredients include diced carrots, peas, onions, shrimp, chicken, and Chinese sausage.

The key to making delicious Chinese Fried Rice is to use cooked rice that has been cooled beforehand.

This helps to ensure that the rice does not become mushy when stir-fried. Additionally, the vegetables and meats should be chopped into small, bite-sized pieces to ensure even cooking. The dish is typically cooked in a wok, which allows for quick and even heating.

Chinese Fried Rice can be enjoyed on its own as a main dish or served as a side dish alongside other Chinese dishes. It is a filling and satisfying meal that can be made quickly and easily, making it a popular choice for busy weeknights. Whether you are a fan of vegetables or meat, there are endless variations of Chinese Fried Rice to suit your taste buds. So why not try your hand at making this delicious and popular Chinese dish today?

In Chinese cuisine, fried rice is not only a popular dish but also a symbol of hospitality and generosity. It is often served to guests and loved ones as a way to show appreciation and respect. In Chinese culture, the preparation and presentation of food are considered an art form, and fried rice is no exception. The dish is not only delicious but also visually appealing, with its colorful ingredients and perfectly cooked grains of rice.

Chinese Fried Rice has a long history that dates back to ancient China. Rice was a staple food in China, and fried rice was a way to make use of leftover rice and other ingredients. The dish was originally made for the lower classes, but over time, it became popular among all classes of society. Today, Chinese Fried Rice can be found in restaurants and homes all over the world, and its popularity shows no signs of slowing down.

In conclusion, Chinese Fried Rice is a delicious and versatile dish that has a long and rich history in Chinese cuisine. It is a dish that has become popular all over the world and can be customized to individual tastes. Whether you prefer it with vegetables or meat, it is a filling and satisfying meal that can be enjoyed on its own or as a side dish. So why not try making your own Chinese Fried Rice and experience the art of Chinese cooking for yourself?

Here is a classic recipe for Fried Rice:

Ingredients for Fried Rice:

- 2 cups cooked rice
- 1 small onion, diced
- 2 cloves garlic, minced

- 1 cup mixed vegetables (carrots, peas, and corn)
- 1 cup diced cooked meat (chicken, beef, or pork)
- 2 eggs, beaten
- 2 tablespoons oil
- 2 tablespoons soy sauce
- Salt and pepper to taste

Here is a list of tools you would need to make Chinese fried rice:

- **Wok or large skillet:** A wok or large skillet is necessary for stir-frying the ingredients, as it provides a large cooking surface and allows the food to cook quickly and evenly.
- **Spatula**: A spatula is needed for stirring and flipping the ingredients in the wok.
- **Rice cooker:** A rice cooker is used to cook the rice, or alternatively, you can cook the rice on the stovetop.
- **Cutting board** and knife: A cutting board and knife are needed for cutting and preparing the vegetables and meat.
- **Measuring cups** and spoons: Measuring cups and spoons are necessary for measuring the ingredients and ensuring consistent results.
- **Bowl:** A bowl is needed for beating the eggs.

- **Serving dish:** A serving dish is needed for serving the fried rice.

This is a basic list of tools needed to make Chinese fried rice, but other kitchen tools, such as a strainer or colander for rinsing the rice, and a large bowl for mixing the ingredients, can also be useful.

Instructions for Fried Rice:

1. Heat oil in a wok or large skillet over medium-high heat.
2. Add the onion and garlic and cook until softened, about 2 minutes.
3. Add the mixed vegetables and cook until they are tender, about 4 minutes.
4. Add the cooked meat and cook until heated through, about 2 minutes.
5. Push the ingredients to one side of the wok and pour the beaten eggs on the other side. Scramble the eggs until cooked, about 2 minutes.
6. Add the cooked rice to the wok and stir to combine with the other ingredients.
7. Stir in the soy sauce, salt, and pepper. Cook for 2-3 minutes, until the rice is heated through.
8. Serve hot.

This is a basic recipe for Chinese fried rice, but feel free to add or modify ingredients to your liking. For example, you can add other vegetables, such as bell peppers or mushrooms, or use different types of meat or seasonings to create a unique flavor. Enjoy!

Egg Fried Noodles:

Chinese Egg Fried Noodles, also known as chow mein, is a popular Chinese dish that is enjoyed around the world. The dish consists of stir-fried noodles that are coated with a savory sauce and mixed with vegetables, meat, and eggs. The noodles used in the dish are typically egg noodles, which are thin, yellow noodles made from wheat flour and eggs. The dish is a versatile one and can be customized according to personal preferences. Common ingredients used in Chinese Egg Fried Noodles include bean sprouts, green onions, carrots, cabbage, shrimp, beef, and chicken.

The key to making delicious Chinese Egg Fried Noodles is to use fresh ingredients and cook them quickly over high heat. The noodles should be cooked just until they are al dente, or firm to the bite. The vegetables should be chopped into small, uniform pieces to ensure even cooking. The dish is typically cooked in a wok, which allows for quick and even heating. The noodles are stir-fried with the vegetables and meats, and then tossed with a savory sauce made from soy sauce, oyster sauce, and other seasonings.

Chinese Egg Fried Noodles is a filling and satisfying dish that can be enjoyed as a main meal or as a side dish. It is a popular street food in China and can be found in many Chinese restaurants around the world. The dish is also a favorite among college students and those looking for a quick and easy meal. It is a great way to use up leftover vegetables and meats, and can be made in just a few minutes.

In Chinese culture, noodles are considered a symbol of longevity and prosperity. The long, unbroken strands of the noodles represent long life, and eating them is thought to bring good luck and fortune. In Chinese cuisine, noodles are often served during special occasions such as birthdays, weddings, and New Year's celebrations. Chinese Egg Fried Noodles is a delicious and festive dish that is often served during these occasions.

Here is a classic recipe for Egg Fried Noodles:

Ingredients:

- 8 ounces noodles (chow mein or lo mein)

- 2 eggs, beaten
- 2 tablespoons oil
- 2 cloves garlic, minced
- 1 small onion, sliced
- 1 cup mixed vegetables (carrots, peas, and bell peppers)
- 2 tablespoons soy sauce
- Salt and pepper to taste

Here is a list of tools you would need to make egg fried noodles:

- **Wok or large skillet:** A wok or large skillet is necessary for stir-frying the ingredients, as it provides a large cooking surface and allows the food to cook quickly and evenly.
- **Spatula:** A spatula is needed for stirring and flipping the ingredients in the wok.
- **Cutting board and knife:** A cutting board and knife are needed for cutting and preparing the vegetables and meat.
- **Measuring cups and spoons:** Measuring cups and spoons are necessary for measuring the ingredients and ensuring consistent results.
- **Bowl:** A bowl is needed for beating the eggs.

- **Colander or strainer:** A colander or strainer is needed for draining the cooked noodles.
- **Serving dish:** A serving dish is needed for serving the egg fried noodles.

This is a basic list of tools needed to make egg fried noodles, but other kitchen tools, such as a large bowl for mixing the ingredients, can also be useful.

Instructions Egg Fried Noodles:

1. Cook the noodles according to package instructions and drain. Set aside.
2. In a separate pan, heat oil over medium-high heat. Add the beaten eggs and scramble until cooked, about 2 minutes. Remove from the pan and set aside.
3. In the same pan, add the garlic and onion and cook until softened, about 2 minutes.
4. Add the mixed vegetables and cook until they are tender, about 4 minutes.
5. Add the cooked noodles and scrambled eggs to the pan and stir to combine with the other ingredients.
6. Stir in the soy sauce, salt, and pepper. Cook for 2-3 minutes, until the noodles are heated through.
7. Serve hot.

This is a basic recipe for Chinese egg fried noodles, but feel free to add or modify ingredients to your liking. For example, you can add other vegetables, such as mushrooms or broccoli, or use different types of meat or seasonings to create a unique flavor. Enjoy!

Sweet and Sour Pork:

Chinese Sweet and Sour Pork is a popular dish in Chinese cuisine that has become a favorite in many countries around the world. The dish consists of tender pieces of pork that are marinated, deep-fried, and then coated with a sweet and tangy sauce made from sugar, vinegar, ketchup, and other seasonings. The sauce gives the dish a unique flavor and is often accompanied by vegetables such as bell peppers, onions, and pineapple chunks.

The key to making delicious Chinese Sweet and Sour Pork is to use fresh ingredients and prepare the pork correctly. The pork should be cut into bite-sized pieces and marinated in a mixture of soy sauce, rice wine, and cornstarch. The marinated pork is then deep-fried until golden brown and crispy. The sauce is made by mixing together sugar, vinegar, ketchup, and other seasonings, and then simmering until it thickens. The vegetables are added to the sauce and cooked until they are tender. The deep-fried pork is then added to the sauce and tossed until coated.

Chinese Sweet and Sour Pork is a popular dish that can be found in many Chinese restaurants around the world. It is often served as a main dish and can be accompanied by steamed rice or noodles. The dish is a favorite among children and adults alike, and is often ordered for special occasions such as birthdays and weddings. It is a filling and satisfying meal that is sure to please any palate.

In Chinese cuisine, Sweet and Sour Pork is considered a classic dish that has a long history. The dish originated in the Guangdong Province of China and was introduced to the United States in the early 20th century. Today, the dish has become a staple in Chinese restaurants around the world and is enjoyed by people of all backgrounds.

Here is a classic recipe for Sweet and sour pork:

Ingredients:

- 1 pound pork loin, cut into 1-inch cubes
- 1 cup all-purpose flour
- 2 eggs, beaten
- 1 cup breadcrumbs

- Oil for frying

- 1 small onion, sliced

- 1 red bell pepper, sliced

- 1 green bell pepper, sliced

- 1 cup pineapple chunks

- 1/4 cup vinegar

- 1/4 cup ketchup

- 1/4 cup sugar

- 2 tablespoons soy sauce

- 1 tablespoon cornstarch

- 2 tablespoons water

Here is a list of tools you would need to make sweet and sour pork:

- **Wok or large skillet:** A wok or large skillet is necessary for stir-frying the ingredients, as it provides a large cooking surface and allows the food to cook quickly and evenly.

- **Spatula:** A spatula is needed for stirring and flipping the ingredients in the wok.

- **Cutting board and knife:** A cutting board and knife are needed for cutting and preparing the pork and vegetables.

- **Measuring cups and spoons:** Measuring cups and spoons are necessary for measuring the ingredients and ensuring consistent results.
- **Bowls:** Bowls are needed for mixing the flour, eggs, and breadcrumbs, and for whisking the sauce ingredients.
- **Colander or strainer:** A colander or strainer is needed for draining the cooked pork.
- **Serving dish:** A serving dish is needed for serving the sweet and sour pork.

This is a basic list of tools needed to make sweet and sour pork, but other kitchen tools, such as a large bowl for mixing the ingredients, can also be useful.

Instructions for Sweet and sour pork:

1. In a large bowl, mix together the flour, eggs, and breadcrumbs. Dip the pork cubes into the mixture, making sure they are well coated.
2. Heat oil in a wok or large skillet over medium-high heat. Add the coated pork cubes and fry until golden brown, about 4-5 minutes. Remove from the pan and set aside.
3. In the same pan, add the onion and bell peppers and cook until softened, about 2-3 minutes.
4. Add the pineapple chunks and cook for 1-2 minutes.

5. In a small bowl, whisk together the vinegar, ketchup, sugar, soy sauce, cornstarch, and water.

6. Add the sauce to the pan and stir until the sauce thickens, about 2-3 minutes.

7. Return the fried pork cubes to the pan and stir until they are coated with the sauce.

8. Serve hot with rice.

This is a simple recipe for sweet and sour pork, but you can add other ingredients, such as carrots or green beans, or adjust the flavors to suit your taste. Enjoy!

Kung Pao Chicken

Chinese Kung Pao Chicken is a popular dish in Chinese cuisine that originated in the Sichuan Province of China. The dish consists of tender pieces of chicken that are stir-fried with vegetables, peanuts, and chili peppers. The dish is named after a famous Sichuan governor named Ding Baozhen, who was also known as Kung Pao. The dish is characterized by its spicy and flavorful taste, which comes from the use of Sichuan peppercorns and chili peppers.

The key to making delicious Chinese Kung Pao Chicken is to use fresh ingredients and cook them quickly over high heat. The chicken should be cut into bite-sized pieces and marinated in a mixture of soy sauce, rice wine, and cornstarch. The vegetables used in the dish are typically bell peppers, onions, and scallions, but can be customized according to personal preferences. The peanuts and chili peppers are added towards the end of cooking, giving the dish a crunchy texture and spicy flavor.

Chinese Kung Pao Chicken is a popular dish that can be found in many Chinese restaurants around the world. It is often served as a main dish and can be accompanied by steamed rice or noodles. The dish is a favorite among those who enjoy spicy food, and is often ordered by those looking for a little kick in their meal. It is a filling and satisfying meal that is sure to please any palate.

In Chinese culture, Kung Pao Chicken is a dish that is associated with wealth and prosperity. The dish is often served during special occasions such as weddings and New Year's celebrations. In addition to its delicious taste, the dish is also thought to bring good luck and fortune to those who eat it.

Here is a classic recipe for Kung Pao Chicken:

Ingredients for Kung Pao Chicken:

- 1 lb boneless, skinless chicken breasts or thighs, cut into bite-sized pieces
- 1 red bell pepper, sliced
- 1 green bell pepper, sliced
- 1/2 cup unsalted, roasted peanuts
- 1/4 cup chopped green onions
- 1 tablespoon cornstarch
- 2 tablespoons vegetable oil
- 3 garlic cloves, minced
- 1 inch ginger, minced
- 2 tablespoons Sichuan peppercorns (optional)
- 2 dried red chilies, chopped
- 2 tablespoons soy sauce
- 2 tablespoons rice vinegar
- 2 tablespoons sugar
- 1 tablespoon hoisin sauce

Here is a list of tools you would need to make Kung Pao Chicken:

- Cutting board and knife for chopping vegetables and chicken

- Measuring cups and spoons for measuring ingredients
- Mixing bowls for mixing the sauce and cornstarch slurry
- Wok or large frying pan for stir-frying
- Spatula or wooden spoon for stirring the ingredients
- Steaming basket or rice cooker for cooking rice (optional)

Note: A wok is traditionally used for Kung Pao Chicken, as it allows for quick, high-heat cooking that is essential for a successful stir-fry. However, a large frying pan can also be used if a wok is not available.

Instructions for Kung Pao Chicken:

1. In a small bowl, mix the cornstarch with 2 tablespoons of water to make a slurry.
2. In a large wok or frying pan, heat the oil over high heat until hot. Add the chicken pieces and stir-fry for 3-4 minutes, until browned and cooked through. Remove the chicken from the pan and set aside.
3. In the same pan, add the garlic, ginger, Sichuan peppercorns (if using), and dried red chilies. Stir-fry for 30 seconds, until fragrant.
4. Add the red and green bell peppers to the pan and stir-fry for 2-3 minutes, until slightly softened.

5. Return the chicken to the pan and add the peanuts, green onions, soy sauce, rice vinegar, sugar, and hoisin sauce. Stir-fry for another 2-3 minutes, until everything is well combined and the sauce has thickened slightly.

6. Add the cornstarch slurry to the pan and stir-fry for another 30 seconds, until the sauce has thickened further.

7. Serve the Kung Pao chicken hot with steamed rice. Enjoy!

Moo Shu Pork

Chinese Moo Shu Pork is a traditional dish that originated in Northern China. The dish consists of thin strips of pork that are stir-fried with vegetables such as cabbage, carrots, and mushrooms, and served with thin pancakes and hoisin sauce. The dish is known for its unique texture and flavor, which comes from the combination of tender pork and crispy vegetables.

The key to making delicious Chinese Moo Shu Pork is to use fresh ingredients and prepare the meat correctly. The pork should be sliced thinly and marinated in a mixture of soy sauce, rice wine, and cornstarch. The vegetables used in the dish are typically cabbage, carrots, and mushrooms, but can be customized according to personal preferences. The vegetables are stir-fried in a wok until tender and then combined with the pork. The dish is then served with thin pancakes and hoisin sauce, which is a sweet and savory sauce made from soybeans, garlic, and spices.

Chinese Moo Shu Pork is a popular dish that can be found in many Chinese restaurants around the world. It is often served as a main dish and can be accompanied by steamed rice or noodles. The dish is a favorite among those who enjoy the combination of meat and vegetables, and is often ordered by those looking for a healthy and flavorful meal. It is a filling and satisfying meal that is sure to please any palate.

In Chinese culture, Moo Shu Pork is considered a traditional dish that has been enjoyed for centuries. The dish is often associated with the spring festival, which is a time of renewal and new beginnings. The dish is thought to symbolize the arrival of spring, as the vegetables used in the dish are typically in season during this time.

Here is a classic recipe for Moo Shu Pork:

Ingredients for Moo Shu Pork:

- 1 lb boneless pork loin or shoulder, sliced into thin strips

- 4-6 large dried Chinese mushrooms, rehydrated and sliced
- 1 cup sliced bamboo shoots
- 4 green onions, sliced into 2-inch pieces
- 4 cloves garlic, minced
- 1 inch fresh ginger, grated
- 4 tablespoons vegetable oil, divided
- 4 tablespoons hoisin sauce
- 2 tablespoons soy sauce
- 2 tablespoons rice vinegar
- 1 tablespoon cornstarch
- 1 tablespoon sugar
- 8-10 thin mandarin pancakes or flour tortillas
- Fresh cilantro leaves, for garnish

To cook Moo Shu Pork, you will need the following kitchen tools:

- Cutting board and knife for chopping vegetables and slicing the pork
- Measuring cups and spoons for measuring ingredients
- Mixing bowls for mixing the sauce
- Wok or large frying pan for stir-frying

- Spatula or wooden spoon for stirring the ingredients
- Rolling pin or wine bottle for rolling out the mandarin pancakes (optional)
- Non-stick pan for cooking the mandarin pancakes (optional)

Note: A wok is traditionally used for Moo Shu Pork, as it allows for quick, high-heat cooking that is essential for a successful stir-fry. However, a large frying pan can also be used if a wok is not available.

Instructions for Moo Shu Pork:

1. In a small bowl, mix the hoisin sauce, soy sauce, rice vinegar, cornstarch, and sugar until well combined.

2. In a large wok or frying pan, heat 2 tablespoons of oil over high heat until hot. Add the pork strips and stir-fry for 3-4 minutes, until browned and cooked through. Remove the pork from the pan and set aside.

3. In the same pan, add 2 more tablespoons of oil and stir-fry the mushrooms, bamboo shoots, green onions, garlic, and ginger for 2-3 minutes, until fragrant and slightly softened.

4. Return the pork to the pan and add the sauce mixture. Stir-fry for another 2-3 minutes, until

everything is well combined and the sauce has thickened slightly.

5. Serve the Moo Shu Pork with the mandarin pancakes or flour tortillas and garnish with fresh cilantro leaves. Enjoy!

Instructions for Mandarin Pancakes:

1. In a large bowl, mix 2 cups of all-purpose flour with 1/2 cup of boiling water and knead into a soft dough.

2. Divide the dough into 8-10 portions and roll each portion into a thin round.

3. Heat a non-stick pan over medium heat and cook each round for 1-2 minutes on each side, until lightly browned.

4. Serve the pancakes hot with the Moo Shu Pork. Enjoy!

Mapo Tofu:

Chinese Mapo Tofu is a traditional Sichuan dish that has gained popularity all over China and the world. The dish is named after a woman named Mrs. Chen, who was nicknamed "Mapo" due to the pockmarks on her face. The dish is made from tofu, ground pork, and a spicy sauce made from Sichuan peppercorns, chili bean paste, and garlic. The dish is characterized by its numbing and spicy flavor, making it a favorite among those who enjoy bold and flavorful food.

The key to making delicious Chinese Mapo Tofu is to use fresh ingredients and to cook them correctly. The tofu used in the dish should be firm and cut into small cubes, while the ground pork should be cooked until it is browned and crispy. The spicy sauce used in the dish is made from a mixture of chili bean paste, garlic, and Sichuan peppercorns, giving the dish its unique and spicy flavor. The dish is usually served with steamed rice and garnished with scallions and cilantro.

Chinese Mapo Tofu is a popular dish that can be found in many Chinese restaurants around the world. It is often served as a main dish and can be accompanied by other Sichuan dishes such as Kung Pao Chicken or Dan Dan Noodles. The dish is a favorite among those who enjoy spicy food, and is often ordered by those looking for a unique and flavorful meal. It is a filling and satisfying meal that is sure to please any palate.

In Chinese culture, Mapo Tofu is considered a traditional Sichuan dish that has been enjoyed for centuries. The dish is thought to have originated from a small restaurant in the Sichuan province, where Mrs.

Chen would cook the dish for her customers. The dish has since become popular all over China and is considered a staple in Sichuan cuisine.

Here is a classic recipe for Mapo Tofu:

Ingredients for Mapo Tofu:

- 1 lb soft tofu, drained and cut into 1-inch cubes
- 1 lb ground pork or beef
- 4 cloves garlic, minced
- 1 inch fresh ginger, grated
- 2 tablespoons vegetable oil
- 2 tablespoons fermented black beans, rinsed and finely chopped
- 2 tablespoons chili paste
- 2 tablespoons doubanjiang (spicy bean paste)
- 2 tablespoons soy sauce
- 2 tablespoons Shaoxing wine or dry sherry
- 2 tablespoons cornstarch mixed with 4 tablespoons water
- 1 tablespoon Sichuan peppercorns, toasted and ground (optional)
- 2 green onions, sliced into 2-inch pieces
- Steamed rice, for serving

To cook Mapo Tofu, you will need the following kitchen tools:

- Cutting board and knife for chopping ginger and garlic
- Measuring cups and spoons for measuring ingredients
- Mixing bowl for mixing the sauce
- Wok or large frying pan for stir-frying
- Spatula or wooden spoon for stirring the ingredients
- Steaming basket or rice cooker for cooking rice (optional)

Note: A wok is traditionally used for Mapo Tofu, as it allows for quick, high-heat cooking that is essential for a successful stir-fry. However, a large frying pan can also be used if a wok is not available.

Instructions for Mapo Tofu:

1. In a large wok or frying pan, heat the oil over high heat until hot. Add the ground pork and stir-fry for 2-3 minutes, until browned and cooked through. Remove the pork from the pan and set aside.

2. In the same pan, add the garlic, ginger, fermented black beans, chili paste, and doubanjiang. Stir-fry for 1-2 minutes, until fragrant.

3. Return the pork to the pan and add the tofu cubes. Gently stir to combine and avoid breaking the tofu.

4. In a small bowl, mix the soy sauce, Shaoxing wine, and cornstarch mixture. Pour the mixture into the pan and stir to combine.

5. Let the sauce simmer for 2-3 minutes, until it has thickened slightly. Stir in the Sichuan peppercorns (if using) and green onions.

6. Serve the Mapo Tofu over steamed rice and enjoy!

Stir-Fried Vegetables

Chinese Stir-Fried Vegetables, also known as chao shucai (炒蔬菜) in Mandarin, is a staple dish in Chinese cuisine that is enjoyed by many people around the world. The dish typically consists of a variety of vegetables, such as broccoli, bok choy, carrots, and mushrooms, stir-fried in a wok with garlic, ginger, soy sauce, and other seasonings. This simple yet flavorful dish is a great way to incorporate healthy vegetables into your diet while enjoying a tasty meal.

The key to making delicious Chinese Stir-Fried Vegetables is to use fresh and high-quality ingredients. Vegetables should be cut into similar-sized pieces to ensure even cooking, and it's important not to overcook them to retain their texture and flavor. A hot wok and quick cooking over high heat help to lock in the nutrients and natural flavors of the vegetables. The dish can be customized to personal preferences, and additional ingredients like meat, tofu, or noodles can be added for a more substantial meal.

Chinese Stir-Fried Vegetables are a popular dish that can be found in many Chinese restaurants and homes around the world. They are often served as a side dish or can be combined with rice or noodles to make a complete meal. The dish is especially popular among vegetarians and those looking for a healthy and delicious meal. It is a great way to add variety and nutrition to your diet while enjoying the bold and savory flavors of Chinese cuisine.

In Chinese culture, stir-frying is a traditional cooking method that has been used for centuries. It is considered an art form, and skilled chefs are revered for their ability to cook dishes quickly and evenly over high heat. Stir-Fried Vegetables are a classic example of this cooking technique and are enjoyed by people of all ages and backgrounds.

Here is a simple recipe for Chinese Stir-fried Vegetables:

Ingredients for Stir-fried Vegetables:

- 2 tablespoons vegetable oil
- 4 cloves garlic, minced
- 1 inch fresh ginger, grated
- 1 red bell pepper, sliced
- 1 yellow bell pepper, sliced
- 1 large carrot, sliced
- 1 head of broccoli, cut into florets
- 1 cup snow peas, trimmed
- 8 oz mushrooms, sliced
- 2 tablespoons soy sauce
- 2 tablespoons oyster sauce
- 2 teaspoons cornstarch mixed with 2 tablespoons water
- Steamed rice, for serving (optional)

To cook stir-fried vegetables, you will need the following kitchen tools:

- Cutting board and knife for chopping and slicing the vegetables

- Measuring cups and spoons for measuring ingredients
- Mixing bowl for mixing the sauce
- Wok or large frying pan for stir-frying
- Spatula or wooden spoon for stirring the ingredients

Note: A wok is traditionally used for stir-frying, as it allows for quick, high-heat cooking that is essential for a successful stir-fry. However, a large frying pan can also be used if a wok is not available.

Instructions stir-fried vegetables:

1. In a large wok or frying pan, heat the oil over high heat until hot. Add the garlic and ginger and stir-fry for 1-2 minutes, until fragrant.
2. Add the bell peppers, carrot, broccoli, snow peas, and mushrooms to the pan and stir-fry for 2-3 minutes, until the vegetables are just tender and still crisp.
3. In a small bowl, mix the soy sauce, oyster sauce, and cornstarch mixture. Pour the mixture into the pan and stir to combine.
4. Let the sauce simmer for 1-2 minutes, until it has thickened slightly.
5. Serve the Stir-fried Vegetables over steamed rice, if desired, and enjoy!

Chinese Scallion Pancakes

Chinese Scallion Pancakes, also known as cong you bing (葱油饼) in Mandarin, are a popular snack and appetizer in Chinese cuisine. The dish is made from a simple dough that is rolled out and filled with scallions, sesame oil, and other seasonings. The pancake is then cooked on a griddle until it is crispy on the outside and tender on the inside. Scallion Pancakes are a delicious and savory treat that can be enjoyed at any time of the day.

The key to making delicious Chinese Scallion Pancakes is to use high-quality ingredients and to follow the recipe closely. The dough should be made from a mixture of flour, water, and salt, and should be kneaded until it is smooth and elastic. The scallions should be chopped finely and mixed with sesame oil, salt, and other seasonings. The pancake should be cooked over medium heat until it is golden brown and crispy on both sides. Scallion Pancakes can be served on their own or with a dipping sauce, such as soy sauce or vinegar.

Chinese Scallion Pancakes are a popular street food in China and can be found in many restaurants and food stalls. They are often served as a snack or appetizer and are sometimes served with other dishes, such as hot and sour soup or stir-fried vegetables. The dish is enjoyed by people of all ages and is a great way to experience the bold and savory flavors of Chinese cuisine.

In Chinese culture, Scallion Pancakes are considered a traditional dish that has been enjoyed for centuries. The dish is believed to have originated in northern China, where it was a popular snack among farmers and laborers. Today, Scallion Pancakes are enjoyed all over China and have become a staple in Chinese cuisine.

Here is a recipe for Chinese Scallion Pancakes:

Ingredients for Chinese Scallion Pancakes:

- 2 cups all-purpose flour
- 1 teaspoon salt
- 1/2 cup boiling water
- 1/2 cup cold water
- 1/2 cup thinly sliced scallions (green onions)
- 2 tablespoons vegetable oil, divided

To cook scallion pancakes, you'll need the following kitchen tools:

1. Mixing bowl: to mix the dough ingredients together.

2. Rolling pin: to roll out the dough into thin circles.

3. Knife: to chop the scallions and divide the dough into portions.

4. Non-stick pan or griddle: to cook the pancakes.

5. Spatula: to flip the pancakes and remove them from the pan.

6. Pastry brush (optional): to brush the pancakes with oil or egg wash before cooking.

7. Cutting board (optional): to chop the scallions.

8. Measuring cups and spoons (optional): to measure out the ingredients accurately.

With these tools, you'll be able to make delicious scallion pancakes at home.

Note: A pastry brush can be useful for brushing the oil onto the dough, but you can also use a clean kitchen cloth or paper towel instead.

Instructions Chinese Scallion Pancakes:

1. In a large mixing bowl, combine the flour and salt. Make a well in the center and pour in the boiling water. Stir with a fork until a rough dough forms.

2. Gradually add the cold water, mixing and kneading until a soft and smooth dough forms, about 5-10

minutes. Place the dough in a bowl, cover with plastic wrap, and let it rest for 30 minutes.

3. Roll the dough out into a large, thin rectangle, about 1/4 inch thick. Brush with 1 tablespoon of oil and sprinkle with the sliced scallions.

4. Roll up the dough tightly, starting from one of the short ends. Pinch the ends to seal and shape into a tight cylinder.

5. Cut the cylinder into 12 equal slices and flatten each slice into a disk. Roll each disk out into a thin round pancake, about 1/8 inch thick.

6. Heat a non-stick frying pan over medium heat. Add 1/2 tablespoon of oil and swirl to coat the bottom of the pan. Cook the pancake for 2-3 minutes on each side, until golden and crispy. Repeat with the remaining pancakes, adding more oil as needed.

7. Serve the Scallion Pancakes hot, either on their own or with a dipping sauce of your choice. Enjoy!

Hot and Sour Soup

Chinese Hot and Sour Soup, also known as suan la tang (酸辣汤) in Mandarin, is a popular soup in Chinese cuisine that is known for its bold and spicy flavors. The soup is made from a combination of broth, meat or tofu, vegetables, and seasonings, including vinegar, soy sauce, and chili oil. Hot and Sour Soup is a delicious and comforting dish that can be enjoyed as a starter or as a main course.

The key to making delicious Chinese Hot and Sour Soup is to use high-quality ingredients and to balance the flavors carefully. The broth can be made from chicken, pork, or vegetable stock, and should be flavored with soy sauce, vinegar, and other seasonings. The soup can be made with meat, such as pork or chicken, or with tofu for a vegetarian option. Vegetables like mushrooms, bamboo shoots, and carrots are commonly used in the soup. The soup should be cooked over low heat until the flavors have melded together and the vegetables are tender.

Chinese Hot and Sour Soup is a popular dish that can be found in many Chinese restaurants around the world. It is often served as a starter or as part of a larger meal, and can be enjoyed throughout the year. The soup is especially popular during the colder months, as it is a comforting and warming dish that can help to soothe a sore throat or clear up congestion.

In Chinese culture, Hot and Sour Soup is considered a traditional dish that has been enjoyed for centuries. It is believed to have originated in the Sichuan province of China, which is known for its bold and spicy cuisine.

Today, Hot and Sour Soup is enjoyed all over China and has become a staple in Chinese cuisine.

Here is a recipe for Hot and Sour Soup:

Ingredients for Hot and Sour Soup:

- 4 cups chicken or vegetable broth
- 1/2 cup sliced shiitake mushrooms
- 1/2 cup diced firm tofu
- 1/4 cup diced bamboo shoots
- 2 tablespoons rice vinegar
- 1 tablespoon soy sauce
- 2 teaspoons sesame oil
- 1 teaspoon cornstarch
- 1 teaspoon sugar
- 1/4 teaspoon white pepper
- 2 large eggs, lightly beaten
- 2 tablespoons thinly sliced scallions (green onions)

Here are the kitchen tools you'll need to cook Hot and Sour Soup:

- Large pot or Dutch oven
- Cutting board
- Chef's knife

- Measuring cups and spoons
- Whisk
- Ladle
- Serving bowls

Note: A strainer can be useful for removing solids from the soup, but it's not strictly necessary.

Instructions for Hot and Sour Soup:

1. In a large pot or Dutch oven, bring the broth to a boil over high heat. Add the shiitake mushrooms, tofu, and bamboo shoots, and reduce the heat to medium. Simmer for 5 minutes, or until the mushrooms are tender.

2. In a small bowl, whisk together the rice vinegar, soy sauce, sesame oil, cornstarch, sugar, and white pepper. Gradually add this mixture to the soup, stirring constantly, until well combined.

3. Reduce the heat to low and slowly drizzle in the beaten eggs, stirring gently with a fork to create ribbons of egg in the soup.

4. Serve the Hot and Sour Soup in bowls, garnished with the scallions. Serve hot. Enjoy!

Steamed Dumplings

Chinese Steamed Dumplings, also known as xiao long bao (小笼包) in Mandarin, are a popular dish in Chinese cuisine that is enjoyed all over the world. The dumplings are made from a thin layer of dough that is filled with meat or vegetables and then steamed until tender and juicy. Steamed Dumplings are a delicious and comforting food that can be enjoyed as a snack or as a main course.

The key to making delicious Chinese Steamed Dumplings is to use high-quality ingredients and to make the dough and filling carefully. The dough should be made from a mixture of flour, water, and salt, and should be kneaded until it is smooth and elastic. The filling can be made from a variety of ingredients, including pork, chicken, beef, shrimp, or vegetables, and should be seasoned with soy sauce, ginger, garlic, and other seasonings. The dumplings should be steamed over high heat until they are cooked through and the filling is tender and juicy.

Chinese Steamed Dumplings are a popular dish that can be found in many Chinese restaurants around the world. They are often served as a snack or as part of a larger meal, and can be enjoyed throughout the year. The dumplings are especially popular during the

Lunar New Year, when they are considered a symbol of prosperity and good luck.

In Chinese culture, Steamed Dumplings are considered a traditional dish that has been enjoyed for centuries. The dish is believed to have originated in the Jiangnan region of China, which is known for its delicate and refined cuisine. Today, Steamed Dumplings are enjoyed all over China and have become a staple in Chinese cuisine.

Here is a recipe for Streamed Dumplings:

Ingredients for Steamed Dumplings:

- 1 cup all-purpose flour
- 1/4 teaspoon salt
- 2 teaspoons baking powder
- 2 tablespoons cold unsalted butter, cut into small pieces
- 2/3 cup warm milk
- Filling of your choice (e.g. ground meat, vegetables, cheese)

Here are the kitchen tools you'll need to cook steamed dumplings:

1. Bamboo steamer: You'll need a bamboo steamer to steam the dumplings. A steaming basket or metal steamer can also be used.

2. Wok or pot: You'll need a wok or pot to boil water for steaming the dumplings.

3. Parchment paper or lettuce leaves: To prevent the dumplings from sticking to the steamer, you can line the steamer with parchment paper or lettuce leaves.

4. Slotted spoon or spatula: To remove the dumplings from the steamer, you'll need a slotted spoon or spatula.

5. Dough scraper: If you're making the dumpling dough from scratch, a dough scraper can be helpful for dividing and shaping the dough.

6. Rolling pin: If you're making the dumpling wrappers from scratch, you'll need a rolling pin to roll out the dough.

7. Filling spoon or small scoop: You'll need a spoon or small scoop to portion the filling for the dumplings.

8. Bowl: You'll need a bowl to hold the dumpling filling and a small bowl for dipping sauce.

9. Plate: You'll need a plate to hold the finished dumplings.

Having these tools on hand will make preparing and steaming dumplings easier and more enjoyable.

Instructions for Steamed Dumplings:

1. In a medium bowl, whisk together the flour, salt, and baking powder.
2. Add the cold butter to the flour mixture and use your fingers or a pastry cutter to mix the butter into the flour until it resembles coarse crumbs.
3. Add the warm milk to the flour mixture and stir until a sticky dough forms.
4. On a lightly floured surface, roll out the dough to 1/8 inch thickness.
5. Use a cookie cutter or a cup to cut circles out of the dough.
6. Place a small amount of filling in the center of each dough circle.
7. Fold the dough over the filling to form a half-moon shape, and press the edges together to seal the dumplings.
8. In a large pot or wok, bring a large pot of water to a boil.

9. Place the dumplings in the boiling water and cook for 2-3 minutes, or until they float to the surface.

10. Remove the dumplings from the water with a slotted spoon and serve with your favorite sauce. Enjoy!

Chow Mein

Chinese Chow Mein is a popular dish in Chinese cuisine that is enjoyed all over the world. The dish is made from stir-fried noodles that are mixed with vegetables, meat, or seafood and seasoned with a variety of sauces and spices. Chow Mein is a versatile dish that can be customized to personal preferences and can be enjoyed as a main course or as a side dish.

The key to making delicious Chinese Chow Mein is to use high-quality ingredients and to cook the noodles and vegetables carefully. The noodles can be made from wheat or rice flour, and should be cooked until they are tender but still slightly firm. The vegetables can be a combination of any kind, such as carrots, cabbage, onions, bean sprouts, and bell peppers, and should be cooked until they are slightly charred but still crisp. The dish can be made with meat, such as chicken, beef, or pork, or with seafood like shrimp or scallops, and should be seasoned with soy sauce, oyster sauce, sesame oil, and other spices.

Chinese Chow Mein is a popular dish that can be found in many Chinese restaurants around the world. It is often served as a main course or as a side dish, and can be enjoyed throughout the year. The dish is especially popular during the Lunar New Year, when it is considered a symbol of prosperity and good luck.

In Chinese culture, Chow Mein is considered a traditional dish that has been enjoyed for centuries. It is believed to have originated in northern China, where wheat noodles are a staple food. Today, Chow Mein is enjoyed all over China and has become a staple in Chinese cuisine.

Here is a recipe for Chow Mein:

Ingredients for Chow Mein:

- 8 oz Chinese egg noodles
- 2 tablespoons oil (vegetable or peanut)
- 2 cloves garlic, minced
- 1 large onion, sliced
- 1 large carrot, sliced
- 1 cup sliced cabbage

Here is a recipe for Szechuan Beef:

Ingredients for Szechuan Beef:

- 1 pound flank steak, thinly sliced against the grain
- 1 cup cornstarch
- 1/4 cup vegetable oil
- 4 cloves garlic, minced
- 1 inch fresh ginger, peeled and minced
- 1/2 cup diced onion
- 1 red bell pepper, thinly sliced
- 1 green bell pepper, thinly sliced
- 1/4 cup Szechuan sauce
- 1/4 cup hoisin sauce
- 2 tablespoons soy sauce
- 2 tablespoons rice vinegar
- 1 tablespoon sugar
- 1 teaspoon red pepper flakes (optional)
- 4 green onions, sliced
- Sesame seeds, for garnish

To cook Szechuan beef, you will need a few essential kitchen tools, including:

1. Wok or a large skillet: You'll need a large, deep wok or skillet to cook the beef and vegetables quickly and evenly.

2. Chef's knife: You'll need a sharp chef's knife to slice the beef and vegetables thinly.

3. Cutting board: You'll need a clean, flat surface to chop and slice the beef and vegetables.

4. Wooden spatula or tongs: A wooden spatula or tongs are useful for stir-frying the beef and vegetables in the wok or skillet.

5. Measuring spoons and cups: Measuring spoons and cups are essential for accurately measuring the ingredients for the sauce.

6. Garlic press: You may need a garlic press to quickly mince garlic for the recipe.

7. Grater: A grater is optional but can be helpful for grating ginger for the recipe.

8. Bowls and plates: You'll need bowls and plates to hold the prepped ingredients and serve the finished dish.

9. Oil strainer: After deep frying the beef, you may need an oil strainer to drain the excess oil.

Having these tools on hand will make preparing Szechuan beef easier and more enjoyable.

Instructions for Szechuan Beef:

1. In a large bowl, mix together the beef and cornstarch until the beef is evenly coated.

2. Heat a large wok or frying pan over high heat. Add the oil and swirl to coat the pan.

3. Once the oil is hot, add the beef in a single layer. Cook for 2-3 minutes on each side, until the beef is browned and crispy. Remove the beef from the pan and set aside on a plate.

4. In the same pan, add the garlic, ginger, and onion. Cook for 1-2 minutes, until the onion is translucent.

5. Add the red and green bell peppers to the pan and cook for an additional 2-3 minutes, until the peppers are soft.

6. In a small bowl, whisk together the Szechuan sauce, hoisin sauce, soy sauce, rice vinegar, sugar, and red pepper flakes (if using).

7. Pour the sauce over the vegetables in the pan, and stir to combine. Cook for 2-3 minutes, until the sauce has thickened.

8. Add the cooked beef back to the pan and stir to coat with the sauce. Cook for an additional 1-2 minutes, until the beef is heated through.

9. Serve the Szechuan beef over steamed rice and sprinkle with green onions and sesame seeds. Enjoy!

Wontons

Chinese Wontons are a type of dumpling that originated in China and are now enjoyed all over the world. Wontons are made from a thin sheet of dough that is filled with a mixture of meat, vegetables, or seafood and then wrapped into small shapes. The dumplings can be boiled, steamed, or fried, and are often served with a dipping sauce.

The key to making delicious Chinese Wontons is to use high-quality ingredients and to prepare the filling carefully. The filling can be made with ground pork, shrimp, chicken, or a combination of different ingredients, and can be seasoned with soy sauce, sesame oil, and other spices. The dough should be rolled thin and cut into small circles, and then the filling should be placed in the center of each circle and wrapped into small shapes.

Chinese Wontons are a popular dish that can be found in many Chinese restaurants around the world. They are often served as a side dish or as an appetizer, and can be enjoyed with a variety of dipping sauces. The dumplings are especially popular during the Lunar New Year, when they are considered a symbol of wealth and prosperity.

In Chinese culture, Wontons are considered a traditional dish that has been enjoyed for centuries. The dumplings are believed to have originated in the Tang Dynasty and have been a popular dish ever since. Today, Wontons are enjoyed all over China and have become a staple in Chinese cuisine.

Here's a basic recipe for making wontons:

Ingredients for Wontons:

- 1 pound ground pork or shrimp
- 1/2 cup finely chopped Napa cabbage
- 1/4 cup finely chopped scallions
- 2 cloves of garlic, minced
- 1 tablespoon soy sauce
- 1 teaspoon sesame oil
- 1/4 teaspoon white pepper
- 40 wonton wrappers

To make wontons, you'll need the following kitchen tools:

1. A large mixing bowl for preparing the filling
2. A cutting board and knife for chopping the ingredients
3. A tablespoon or teaspoon measure for portioning the filling
4. A small bowl of water for dampening the edges of the wonton wrappers
5. A clean work surface for assembling the wontons
6. A pot or large saucepan for boiling the wontons, or a frying pan for frying them
7. A slotted spoon or strainer for removing the wontons from boiling water or hot oil
8. A serving plate for presenting the cooked wontons.

Some additional optional tools that might make the process easier include a food processor for grinding the filling ingredients, a rolling pin for rolling out the wonton wrappers, and a wonton press for quickly and easily sealing the wontons. However, these are not essential and can be replaced with a manual method like using your fingers to crimp the edges of the wontons.

Instructions for Wontons:

1. In a large bowl, mix together the ground pork or shrimp, cabbage, scallions, garlic, soy sauce, sesame oil, and white pepper.

2. Place a wrapper on a clean surface and spoon about 1 teaspoon of the filling into the center.

3. Dip your fingers in water and wet the edges of the wrapper.

4. Fold the wrapper in half to form a triangle and press the edges together to seal.

5. Bring the two opposite corners of the triangle together and press to seal, forming a wonton shape. Repeat with the remaining wrappers and filling.

6. To cook the wontons, you can either boil them in a pot of salted water for 2-3 minutes or until they float to the surface, or fry them in a pan with hot oil until they are golden brown.

7. Serve the wontons hot with your favorite dipping sauce, such as soy sauce or sweet chili sauce.

Note: You can also experiment with different filling ingredients to create unique flavors. For example, you could use a mixture of ground chicken, mushrooms, and ginger for a different take on the classic wonton filling.

Mongolian Beef

Chinese Mongolian Beef is a popular dish in Chinese cuisine that originated in Northern China. The dish is made from thinly sliced beef that is stir-fried with a savory and slightly sweet sauce made from soy sauce, hoisin sauce, garlic, ginger, and brown sugar. The dish is known for its tender beef and rich flavors, making it a favorite among Chinese food lovers.

The key to making delicious Mongolian Beef is to use high-quality ingredients and to slice the beef thinly against the grain. The beef should be marinated for at least 30 minutes to enhance its flavor and tenderness. The sauce can be made by combining soy sauce, hoisin sauce, garlic, ginger, brown sugar, and other seasonings and then stir-frying it with the beef and vegetables.

Chinese Mongolian Beef is a popular dish that can be found in many Chinese restaurants around the world. It is often served as a main course and can be enjoyed with rice or noodles. The dish is especially popular among those who enjoy sweet and savory flavors and is a favorite among fans of Chinese cuisine.

In Chinese culture, Mongolian Beef is considered a traditional dish that has been enjoyed for centuries. It is believed to have originated in the Northern region of China, which is known for its hearty and flavorful dishes. Today, Mongolian Beef is enjoyed all over China and has become a staple in Chinese cuisine.

Here's a recipe for making Mongolian beef:

Ingredients for Mongolian Beef:

- 1 pound flank steak or sirloin, sliced thin
- 1/4 cup cornstarch
- 1/4 cup vegetable oil
- 3 cloves of garlic, minced
- 1 tablespoon grated ginger
- 1/4 cup soy sauce
- 1/4 cup hoisin sauce
- 1/4 cup brown sugar
- 1/4 cup water
- 2 green onions, sliced
- Steamed white rice, for serving

To make Mongolian beef, you will need the following kitchen tools:

1. A large mixing bowl for coating the beef in cornstarch
2. A cutting board and knife for slicing the beef and green onions
3. Measuring cups and spoons for measuring the ingredients
4. A large frying pan or wok for stir-frying the beef and sauce
5. A wooden spoon or spatula for stirring the ingredients in the pan
6. A small bowl for mixing the sauce ingredients
7. A serving platter or bowls for serving the finished dish.

Note: A wok is typically used for stir-frying dishes like Mongolian beef because of its high, sloping sides and ability to heat evenly. If you don't have a wok, a large frying pan can be used as an alternative.

Instructions for Mongolian Beef:

1. Place the sliced beef in a bowl and add the cornstarch. Toss until the beef is coated in cornstarch.

2. Heat the oil in a large frying pan or wok over high heat. Add the beef to the pan and stir-fry for 2-3 minutes, or until browned and crispy. Remove the beef from the pan and set aside.

3. In the same pan, add the garlic and ginger and stir-fry for 30 seconds.

4. In a small bowl, mix together the soy sauce, hoisin sauce, brown sugar, and water. Add the sauce to the pan with the garlic and ginger and stir until the sugar has dissolved.

5. Return the beef to the pan and stir to coat in the sauce. Cook for an additional 2-3 minutes, or until the sauce has thickened.

6. Serve the Mongolian beef over a bed of steamed white rice, garnished with sliced green onions.

Enjoy your delicious and flavorful Mongolian beef!

Beef and Broccoli

Chinese Beef and Broccoli is a classic Chinese-American dish that is loved by many. The dish features tender strips of beef stir-fried with broccoli in a savory brown sauce. It is a simple yet satisfying dish that is perfect for those who enjoy the combination of meat and vegetables.

The key to making delicious Beef and Broccoli is to use high-quality ingredients and to prepare them carefully. The beef should be thinly sliced against the grain and marinated for at least 30 minutes to enhance its flavor and tenderness. The broccoli should be lightly blanched before being stir-fried with the beef to ensure that it remains crisp and retains its bright green color.

Chinese Beef and Broccoli is a popular dish that can be found in many Chinese restaurants around the world. It is often served as a main course and can be enjoyed with rice or noodles. The dish is especially popular among those who enjoy the combination of meat and vegetables and is a favorite among fans of Chinese cuisine.

In Chinese culture, Beef and Broccoli is considered a traditional dish that has been enjoyed for centuries. While the dish has evolved over time and has been adapted to suit the tastes of different regions, it remains a popular and beloved dish in Chinese cuisine.

Here's a recipe for making Beef and Broccoli:

Ingredients for Beef and Broccoli:

- 1 pound flank steak or sirloin, sliced thin

- 1 head of broccoli, cut into florets
- 1/4 cup cornstarch
- 1/4 cup vegetable oil
- 3 cloves of garlic, minced
- 1 tablespoon grated ginger
- 1/4 cup soy sauce
- 1/4 cup oyster sauce
- 1 tablespoon hoisin sauce
- 1 tablespoon brown sugar
- 1/4 cup water
- 2 green onions, sliced
- Steamed white rice, for serving

To make Beef and Broccoli, you will need the following kitchen tools:

1. A cutting board and knife for slicing the beef and cutting the broccoli
2. A large mixing bowl for coating the beef in cornstarch
3. Measuring cups and spoons for measuring the ingredients
4. A large frying pan or wok for stir-frying the beef and vegetables

5. A wooden spoon or spatula for stirring the ingredients in the pan

6. A small bowl for mixing the sauce ingredients

7. A colander or strainer for blanching the broccoli

8. A serving platter or bowls for serving the finished dish.

Note: A wok is typically used for stir-frying dishes like Beef and Broccoli because of its high, sloping sides and ability to heat evenly. If you don't have a wok, a large frying pan can be used as an alternative.

Instructions for Beef and Broccoli:

1. Place the sliced beef in a bowl and add the cornstarch. Toss until the beef is coated in cornstarch.

2. Blanch the broccoli florets in boiling water for 1-2 minutes, or until bright green and crisp-tender. Drain and set aside.

3. Heat the oil in a large frying pan or wok over high heat. Add the beef to the pan and stir-fry for 2-3 minutes, or until browned and crispy. Remove the beef from the pan and set aside.

4. In the same pan, add the garlic and ginger and stir-fry for 30 seconds.

5. In a small bowl, mix together the soy sauce, oyster sauce, hoisin sauce, brown sugar, and water. Add

the sauce to the pan with the garlic and ginger and stir until the sugar has dissolved.

6. Return the beef to the pan and stir to coat in the sauce. Add the blanched broccoli and continue to stir-fry for an additional 2-3 minutes, or until the sauce has thickened and the vegetables are heated through.

7. Serve the beef and broccoli over a bed of steamed white rice, garnished with sliced green onions.

Enjoy your delicious and flavorful Beef and Broccoli dish!

Shrimp with lobster sauce

Shrimp with Lobster Sauce is a classic Chinese-American dish that has become a staple in many Chinese restaurants around the world. Despite its name, the dish does not actually contain lobster but instead is made with a savory and slightly sweet sauce that resembles the sauce used in lobster dishes. The dish features large shrimp that are stir-fried with a sauce made from ground pork, garlic, ginger, black bean sauce, and chicken broth.

The key to making delicious Shrimp with Lobster Sauce is to use high-quality ingredients and to prepare them carefully. The shrimp should be deveined and peeled before being stir-fried with the sauce. The sauce should be made by first stir-frying ground pork with garlic, ginger, and black bean sauce and then adding chicken broth and cornstarch to thicken the sauce. The dish is often garnished with green onions and served with rice.

Shrimp with Lobster Sauce is a popular dish that is enjoyed by many people around the world. It is often served as a main course and can be enjoyed with rice or noodles. The dish is especially popular among those who enjoy the combination of shrimp and savory flavors and is a favorite among fans of Chinese cuisine.

In Chinese culture, Shrimp with Lobster Sauce is considered a traditional dish that has been enjoyed for centuries. The dish is believed to have originated in the Guangdong province of China, which is known for its seafood dishes. Today, Shrimp with Lobster Sauce is enjoyed all over China and has become a staple in Chinese cuisine.

Here is a recipe for making Shrimp with Lobster Sauce:

Ingredients for Shrimp with Lobster sauce:

- 1 pound large shrimp, peeled and deveined

- 2 tablespoons vegetable oil
- 3 cloves of garlic, minced
- 1 tablespoon grated ginger
- 2 green onions, sliced
- 1 cup chicken broth
- 1/4 cup soy sauce
- 1/4 cup oyster sauce
- 1 tablespoon cornstarch
- 1 tablespoon water
- 1 tablespoon sugar
- 1/4 teaspoon white pepper
- Steamed white rice, for serving

To cook Shrimp with Lobster Sauce, you will need the following kitchen tools:

1. A cutting board and knife for chopping the green onions and ginger
2. A small bowl for mixing the sauce ingredients
3. Measuring cups and spoons for measuring the ingredients
4. A large frying pan or wok for stir-frying the shrimp and sauce
5. A wooden spoon or spatula for stirring the ingredients in the pan

6. A serving platter or bowls for serving the finished dish

7. A strainer or colander for draining the shrimp after cooking.

Note: A wok is typically used for stir-frying dishes like Shrimp with Lobster Sauce because of its high, sloping sides and ability to heat evenly. If you don't have a wok, a large frying pan can be used as an alternative.

Instructions for Shrimp with Lobster sauce:

1. In a small bowl, mix together the chicken broth, soy sauce, oyster sauce, cornstarch, water, sugar, and white pepper. Set aside.

2. Heat the oil in a large frying pan or wok over high heat. Add the shrimp to the pan and stir-fry for 2-3 minutes, or until pink and cooked through. Remove the shrimp from the pan and set aside.

3. In the same pan, add the garlic and ginger and stir-fry for 30 seconds. Add the green onions and stir-fry for an additional 30 seconds.

4. Pour the sauce mixture into the pan and stir until the sugar has dissolved.

5. Return the shrimp to the pan and stir to coat in the sauce. Cook for an additional 1-2 minutes, or until

the sauce has thickened and the shrimp are heated through.

6. Serve the Shrimp with Lobster Sauce over a bed of steamed white rice.

Enjoy your delicious and flavorful Shrimp with Lobster Sauce dish!

Cashew Chicken

Chinese Cashew Chicken is a popular Chinese-American dish that has become a favorite of many people around the world. The dish features tender pieces of chicken that are stir-fried with vegetables and cashew nuts in a savory brown sauce. It is a simple yet satisfying dish that is perfect for those who enjoy the combination of meat, vegetables, and nuts.

The key to making delicious Cashew Chicken is to use high-quality ingredients and to prepare them carefully. The chicken should be cut into bite-sized pieces and marinated in a mixture of soy sauce, rice wine, and cornstarch to enhance its flavor and tenderness. The vegetables should be cut into uniform pieces and stir-fried quickly to ensure that they remain crisp and retain their bright colors.

Cashew Chicken is a popular dish that can be found in many Chinese restaurants around the world. It is often served as a main course and can be enjoyed with rice or noodles. The dish is especially popular among those who enjoy the combination of meat, vegetables, and nuts and is a favorite among fans of Chinese cuisine.

In Chinese culture, Cashew Chicken is considered a modern dish that was created in the United States in the 1960s. Despite its modern origins, the dish has become a favorite of many people and has been adapted to suit the tastes of different regions. Today, Cashew Chicken is enjoyed all over the world and has become a staple in Chinese cuisine.

Here is a recipe for making Cashew Chicken:

Ingredients for Cashew Chicken:

- 1 pound boneless, skinless chicken breast, diced
- 1 cup roasted cashews
- 1 red bell pepper, diced
- 1 green bell pepper, diced
- 1 onion, diced
- 2 tablespoons vegetable oil
- 2 cloves of garlic, minced

- 1 tablespoon grated ginger
- 1/4 cup chicken broth
- 2 tablespoons soy sauce
- 2 tablespoons oyster sauce
- 2 tablespoons hoisin sauce
- 1 tablespoon cornstarch
- 1 tablespoon water
- Steamed white rice, for serving

To cook Cashew Chicken, you will need the following kitchen tools:

1. A cutting board and knife for chopping the chicken, bell peppers, onion, ginger, and garlic
2. Measuring cups and spoons for measuring the ingredients
3. A large frying pan or wok for stir-frying the chicken and vegetables
4. A wooden spoon or spatula for stirring the ingredients in the pan
5. A serving platter or bowls for serving the finished dish
6. A small bowl for mixing the sauce ingredients.

Note: A wok is typically used for stir-frying dishes like Cashew Chicken because of its high, sloping sides and ability to heat evenly. If you don't have a wok, a large frying pan can be used as an alternative

Instructions for Cashew Chicken

1. In a small bowl, mix together the chicken broth, soy sauce, oyster sauce, hoisin sauce, cornstarch, and water. Set aside.

2. Heat the oil in a large frying pan or wok over high heat. Add the chicken to the pan and stir-fry for 2-3 minutes, or until browned and cooked through. Remove the chicken from the pan and set aside.

3. In the same pan, add the garlic and ginger and stir-fry for 30 seconds. Add the red and green bell peppers and onion and stir-fry for an additional 2-3 minutes, or until the vegetables are tender.

4. Return the chicken to the pan and add the cashews. Stir in the sauce mixture and cook for an additional 2-3 minutes, or until the sauce has thickened and the chicken is heated through.

5. Serve the Cashew Chicken over a bed of steamed rice.

Enjoy your delicious and flavorful Cashew Chicken dish!

Yangzhou Fried Rice

Yangzhou Fried Rice, also known as Yeung Chow Fried Rice, is a popular Chinese dish that originated in the city of Yangzhou in the Jiangsu Province of China. The dish is made with long-grain rice that is stir-fried with vegetables, eggs, and meat, typically ham, shrimp, and chicken. The resulting dish is flavorful and fragrant, with a slightly sweet and savory taste that is irresistible.

The key to making delicious Yangzhou Fried Rice is to use high-quality ingredients and to cook them carefully. The rice should be cooked just right, neither too soft nor too firm, and allowed to cool before being used in the dish. The vegetables should be finely chopped and stir-fried quickly to retain their crispness and color. The meat should be thinly sliced and marinated in a mixture of soy sauce, rice wine, and cornstarch to enhance its flavor and tenderness.

Yangzhou Fried Rice is a popular dish that can be found in many Chinese restaurants around the world. It is often served as a side dish or main course and can be enjoyed with a variety of other dishes. The dish is especially popular among those who enjoy the combination of meat, vegetables, and rice and is a favorite among fans of Chinese cuisine.

In Chinese culture, Yangzhou Fried Rice is considered a classic dish that has been enjoyed for centuries. The dish is named after the city of Yangzhou, which was known for its rich culinary traditions and was a center of trade and commerce during ancient times. Today, Yangzhou Fried Rice is enjoyed all over the world and has become a staple in Chinese cuisine.

Here is a simple recipe for Yangzhou Fried Rice:

Ingredients for Yangzhou Fried Rice:

- 4 cups cooked long-grain rice (preferably cooled overnight)
- 2 eggs, lightly beaten
- 1/2 cup cooked and diced ham (or other protein like shrimp or chicken)
- 1/2 cup diced carrots
- 1/2 cup frozen peas
- 2 green onions, thinly sliced
- 2 tablespoons vegetable oil
- 1 tablespoon soy sauce
- 1/2 teaspoon salt

- 1/4 teaspoon white pepper

To cook Yangzhou Fried Rice, you will need the following kitchen tools:

1. Wok or large skillet: This is the main cooking vessel for stir-frying the rice and other ingredients.

2. Spatula: A spatula with a flat surface is ideal for stir-frying and breaking up the clumps of rice.

3. Cutting board and knife: You will need a cutting board and a sharp knife to dice the vegetables and protein.

4. Bowls: Bowls are handy for holding the beaten eggs and the diced vegetables and protein before cooking.

5. Measuring spoons and cups: You will need measuring spoons to accurately measure the salt, white pepper, and soy sauce, and measuring cups for the rice.

6. Stove: You will need a stove to cook the fried rice on.

7. Optional: If you prefer your fried rice to have smaller bits of ingredients, you can use a food processor to mince the vegetables and protein beforehand.

Instructions for Yangzhou Fried Rice:

1. Heat a wok or large skillet over high heat. Add 1 tablespoon of oil and swirl to coat.

2. Add the beaten eggs and stir until scrambled and just set. Remove from the wok and set aside.

3. Add another tablespoon of oil to the wok and swirl to coat. Add the diced ham, carrots, and peas and stir-fry for 2-3 minutes, until the vegetables are tender.

4. Add the rice, soy sauce, salt, and white pepper to the wok and stir-fry for 2-3 minutes, breaking up any clumps of rice with a spatula.

5. Add the scrambled eggs and sliced green onions to the wok and stir-fry for another minute or two, until everything is heated through.

6. Serve hot and enjoy!

Note: Feel free to adjust the ingredients and seasoning to your taste. You can also add other vegetables, such as corn or bell peppers, to the dish.

Beef Stir-Fry with Noodles

Beef Stir-Fry with Noodles is a popular dish in Chinese cuisine that features tender strips of beef, vegetables, and stir-fried noodles. The dish is a perfect balance of flavors and textures, with the savory taste of the beef complemented by the crunchy vegetables and soft noodles. The key to making a great beef stir-fry with noodles is to use high-quality ingredients and to cook them quickly and carefully to retain their freshness and flavor.

To make Chinese Beef Stir-Fry with Noodles, you will need a variety of vegetables such as bell peppers, mushrooms, and onions, which are cut into small pieces and stir-fried in a wok along with the beef. The beef is marinated in a mixture of soy sauce, ginger, garlic, and cornstarch to tenderize and flavor it. The noodles are cooked separately and then added to the wok along with the vegetables and beef. The dish is seasoned with a combination of soy sauce, oyster sauce, and sesame oil to give it a rich and savory flavor.

Chinese Beef Stir-Fry with Noodles is a versatile dish that can be customized to your liking. You can use different types of noodles such as egg noodles or udon noodles, and you can also experiment with different vegetables and sauces to create a variety of flavors. The dish is a great way to enjoy the flavors of Chinese cuisine and is a popular choice in Chinese restaurants around the world.

In Chinese culture, stir-fry dishes are considered

healthy and nutritious, as they are cooked quickly and retain the freshness of the ingredients. Chinese Beef Stir-Fry with Noodles is no exception, as it is packed with protein, vegetables, and complex carbohydrates. The dish is a great choice for those looking for a satisfying and healthy meal that is easy to prepare and cook.

Here is a simple recipe for beef stir-fry with noodles:

Ingredients for Beef Stir-Fry with Noodles:

- 8 oz. flank steak, thinly sliced against the grain
- 8 oz. fresh egg noodles
- 2 cups of mixed vegetables (such as bell peppers, onions, and broccoli)
- 3 cloves of garlic, minced
- 1 tablespoon of fresh ginger, grated
- 2 tablespoons of vegetable oil
- 1 tablespoon of soy sauce
- 1 tablespoon of oyster sauce
- 1/4 teaspoon of black pepper
- Salt, to taste

To cook beef stir-fry with noodles, you will need the following kitchen tools:

1. Wok or large skillet: This is the main cooking vessel for stir-frying the beef, vegetables, and noodles.

2. Tongs or spatula: You will need tongs or a spatula with a flat surface to stir-fry the beef and to flip the noodles.

3. Large pot: You will need a large pot to cook the noodles.

4. Colander: A colander is necessary to drain the cooked noodles.

5. Cutting board and knife: You will need a cutting board and a sharp knife to slice the beef and vegetables.

6. Bowls: Bowls are handy for holding the prepared ingredients before cooking and for serving the finished dish.

7. Measuring spoons and cups: You will need measuring spoons to accurately measure the soy sauce, oyster sauce, black pepper, and salt, and measuring cups for the noodles.

8. Grater: You will need a grater to grate the ginger.

9. Optional: If you prefer your vegetables to be cut into uniform shapes, you may want to use a vegetable peeler or a mandoline slicer. Additionally, a garlic

press can be used to mince the garlic instead of chopping it.

Instructions for Beef Stir-Fry with Noodles:

1. Cook the egg noodles according to the package instructions. Drain, rinse with cold water and set aside.

2. In a small bowl, mix together the soy sauce, oyster sauce, and black pepper. Set aside.

3. Heat a wok or a large skillet over high heat. Add the vegetable oil and swirl to coat.

4. Add the beef and stir-fry for 1-2 minutes until browned. Remove from the wok and set aside.

5. Add the mixed vegetables, garlic, and ginger to the wok and stir-fry for 2-3 minutes until the vegetables are tender.

6. Add the beef back into the wok, along with the noodles and the sauce. Stir-fry everything together for another 1-2 minutes until the sauce is well combined and the beef is cooked to your liking.

7. Taste and adjust seasoning with salt, if needed.

8. Serve hot and enjoy!

Note: You can customize the vegetables used in this recipe according to your preference. Other vegetables such as mushrooms, snow peas or carrots can also be used. You can also adjust the amount of sauce to your taste, or add more spice with chili flakes or sriracha.

Spring Rolls

Spring rolls are a popular appetizer that are made by wrapping a mixture of vegetables, meat, and/or seafood in a thin dough wrapper, which is then deep-fried or baked until crispy. The filling can vary, but often includes ingredients such as cabbage, carrots, mushrooms, bean sprouts, tofu, shrimp, or chicken. Spring rolls can be served as an appetizer or a snack, and are typically accompanied by a dipping sauce, such as sweet chili sauce or soy sauce. They can be found in both vegetarian and non-vegetarian varieties.

Here is a simple recipe for Chinese Spring Rolls:

Ingredients for Spring Rolls:

- 12 spring roll wrappers
- 1 cup shredded cabbage
- 1 cup shredded carrots
- 1 cup thinly sliced shiitake mushrooms
- 1 cup bean sprouts
- 1/2 cup chopped green onions

- 2 cloves garlic, minced

- 1 teaspoon grated ginger

- 2 tablespoons soy sauce

- 1 tablespoon sesame oil

- 1 tablespoon cornstarch

- Oil for frying

To cook Chinese spring rolls, you will need some basic kitchen tools:

1. A cutting board and knife for chopping the vegetables and other ingredients

2. A mixing bowl for mixing the filling ingredients

3. A small bowl for whisking the egg to use as a glue for the spring roll wrapper

4. A baking sheet lined with parchment paper for baking the spring rolls

5. A pastry brush for brushing the spring rolls with oil

6. A kitchen brush or spray bottle for lightly misting or brushing the spring rolls with water to keep them moist

7. A clean, flat work surface for assembling the spring rolls

8. Spring roll wrappers

9. Filling ingredients, such as vegetables, meat, noodles, or other desired ingredients

10. Cooking oil for brushing the spring rolls before baking.

Note: Some people prefer to deep-fry their spring rolls, which would require a deep fryer or a deep pot filled with hot oil, a slotted spoon or spider for removing the spring rolls from the oil, and a wire rack or paper towel to drain and cool the spring rolls.

Instructions for Spring Rolls:

1. In a large bowl, combine the cabbage, carrots, shiitake mushrooms, bean sprouts, green onions, garlic, and ginger.

2. In a small bowl, whisk together the soy sauce, sesame oil, and cornstarch. Pour the mixture over the vegetable spring tr mixture and toss to coat.

3. Lay a spring roll wrapper on a flat surface and place about 2 tablespoons of the vegetable filling in the center. Roll the wrapper tightly around the filling, tucking in the sides as you go. Repeat with the remaining wrappers and filling.

4. Heat about 1 inch of oil in a large skillet over medium-high heat. Once hot, carefully add the spring rolls and fry until golden brown and crispy,

about 3-4 minutes per side.

5. Remove the spring rolls from the oil with a slotted spoon and transfer to a paper towel-lined plate to drain.

6. Serve the spring rolls hot with your favorite dipping sauce.

Enjoy your homemade Chinese Spring Rolls!

Final thoughts on Chinese cooking

Chinese cooking is one of the most diverse and popular cuisines in the world, with a rich history that spans thousands of years. From the spicy flavors of Sichuan cuisine to the delicate tastes of Cantonese cuisine, there is something for everyone in the world of Chinese cooking.

One of the most important aspects of Chinese cooking is the emphasis on balance and harmony. This is seen in the use of ingredients that balance flavors and textures, such as the pairing of sweet and sour, or crispy and soft. It is also reflected in the focus on using fresh, seasonal ingredients and creating dishes that are not only delicious but also visually appealing.

Chinese cooking techniques are also unique and varied, with stir-frying, steaming, and braising being just a few examples. These techniques allow for the retention of nutrients and flavors, resulting in healthy and tasty dishes that are full of depth and complexity.

With the rise of globalization, Chinese cooking has become more accessible to people all over the world. In addition to traditional Chinese restaurants, there are now many fusion restaurants that combine Chinese flavors with other cuisines, as well as a wealth of online resources and cookbooks that offer step-by-step instructions for making authentic Chinese dishes at home.

In conclusion, Chinese cooking is a fascinating and delicious culinary tradition that offers a wide variety of flavors, techniques, and ingredients. Whether you are a beginner or an experienced cook, there is always something new to discover and enjoy in the world of Chinese cuisine. So, go ahead and explore this fascinating cuisine and discover the wonders of Chinese cooking for yourself!

Recommended resources.

Below is a list of essential kitchen tools you will need to prepare and cook Chinese cuisine with ease and authenticity. These tools will help you achieve the desired flavors and textures of your favorite Chinese dishes, and make your cooking experience more enjoyable and efficient. (Get more information by scanning the QR code)

- Wok

- Wok Spatula and Ladle

- Rice cooker

- Steamer basket

 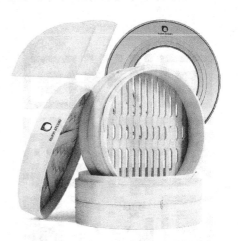

- **Cleaver Knife**

- **Cutting board**

- ## Chopsticks

 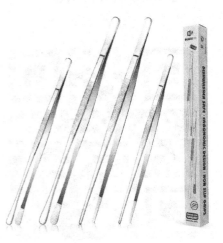

- ## Spatula

- **Measuring cups**

- **Colander**

- Serving dish

- Non-stick frying pan

- **Whisk**

- **Dough scraper**

- **Deep Fryer with Basket**

- **Bowl**

- Wooden cooking spoon set

- Mixing bowl set

Made in the USA
Monee, IL
10 November 2023

46229028R00075